THE PARABLES OF JESUS

Cover image by Clotilde Perrin
Cover design by Bayard Jeunesse
Book design by Bayard Jeunesse

Originally published as *Les paraboles de Jésus*, copyright © 2015 by Bayard Jeunesse

English translation copyright © 2018 by Paulist Press. Translated by Gloria Capik and Ola Czajkowski.

Library of Congress Control Number: 2017942368

ISBN 978-0-8091-6781-4 (hardcover)
ISBN 978-1-58768-740-2 (e-book)

Published by Paulist Press
997 Macarthur Boulevard
Mahwah, New Jersey 07430

www.paulistpress.com

Printed and bound in the
United States of America

The Parables of Jesus

Written by
Bénédicte Jeancourt-Galignani, Marie Aubinais, Gwénaëlle Boulet,
Geoffrey-Kamen Defebvre, Anne-Sophie Du Bouëtiez,
Anne-Laure Fournier Le Ray

Illustrated by
Clotilde Perrin

Paulist Press
New York / Mahwah, NJ

In this book, you will learn about the parables. These are simple stories that Jesus told to his friends to help them better understand who God is. These stories use comparisons with everyday life in Jesus's time. They were easier to understand than long speeches!

But today, these stories are not always very clear to us. Because the world has changed, the images that Jesus used are sometimes hard to understand.

But don't worry! This book explains everything to you with very simple words. The Lost Sheep, the Prodigal Son, the Good Samaritan...these are stories from the Gospels. In this book, the Word of God will open up to you like a treasure.

Happy reading!

Bénédicte Jeancourt-Galignani

What is a parable?

A parable is a story filled with images that people can understand. Parables use simple words and describe everyday situations. But these are not bedtime stories to put children to sleep. They help us understand things that are complicated. They help us think of greater things.

An image of God's love

The parables in this book were told by Jesus. In his time, many people used parables as a way to teach others. The rabbis, who taught Jewish law, also spoke in parables. But Jesus didn't use these stories to explain the law to people. Instead, he was inviting them to become closer to God. He told these parables to help people question things, and to not be set on one way of imagining God. Jesus wanted to challenge people, to have them talk to each other, and to move them. He wanted to put them on the path to God.

Have a nice trip!

The parables of Jesus will inspire you to think, too. You will be surprised, amazed, even angered, and then reassured by reading these stories. They will speak to you, in their own way, of God and his love. They will also invite you to set off on a journey. The most important thing you will discover is that in every story that Jesus told, there is a little bit of you, a little bit of others, and a lot of God.

Contents

Introduction   6
Geoffrey-Kamen Defebvre

The Sower   10
Anne-Sophie Du Bouëtiez

The Lost Sheep   16
Bénédicte Jeancourt-Galignani

The Two Houses   22
Anne-Sophie Du Bouëtiez

The Humble and the Pretentious   28
Marie Aubinais

Sharing Talents   34
Bénédicte Jeancourt-Galignani

The Prodigal Son   40
Anne-Sophie Du Bouëtiez

The Good Samaritan   46
Anne-Laure Fournier Le Ray

The Last-Minute Workers   52
Anne-Laure Fournier Le Ray

Salt and Light   58
Gwénaëlle Boulez

The Sower

From the Gospel according to Saint Mark, chapter 4, verses 2-9

A large crowd came together
to hear Jesus talk about God.
He told this story...

Listen. A sower went out to sow.
Some seeds fell on the side of the road,
and the birds were eager to eat them.
Other seeds fell among the pebbles,
where there was little soil.
They sprouted and grew immediately,
but the sun dried them up.

12

Other seeds fell into the brambles.
As they grew, thorns choked them, and they produced nothing.
But some seeds fell on fertile ground. They sprouted and grew
and they produced beautiful stalks of wheat. Some seeds produced
thirty stalks, others sixty, others a hundred!
Let he who has ears listen...

In the crowd there was
a great silence...

With this parable, Jesus invites everyone who listens to him to be the soil that let's the Word of God bear fruit.

Grain for everyone

In this parable, the sower is Jesus. The seed he sows is the Word of God. We are the land where the seeds are planted. The side of the road, the stones, and the thorns do not represent bad people who shut out his Word. At certain moments in life, anyone can be full of thorns, and at other moments, be fertile ground that yields fruit.

The Living Word

Jesus uses various images to explain to us why the Word of God is not always heard. Sometimes we hear it, but we don't pay enough attention to it because we are too busy. At other times, we don't hear it at all, because we are too angry or rebellious. But sometimes, we feel like we are hearing the Word of God for the first time, as if it was spoken personally to us.

Bearing fruit

Like the seed that sprouts from deep within, the Word is there to awaken something new in us. By taking in the Word of God, some people become actual sources of it, like a stalk of wheat full of seeds. They may keep a low profile, but the work they do in the world is immense. With this parable, Jesus tells us that by listening to the Word of God with an attentive ear, we can all accomplish things that are far beyond our abilities.

The Lost Sheep

From the Gospel according to Saint Luke, chapter 15, verses 1-7

In the crowd of people listening to Jesus, there were people who did not follow the Jewish law very well. This was not pleasing to religious men like the Pharisees and the scribes.

Then Jesus told them this story:

A man owned a herd of a hundred sheep. One morning at dawn, he realized one of them was missing. She had disappeared.

Without delay, the man left his flock in the fields and started looking for the missing sheep. He searched for her, moving heaven and earth, until he found her again. When he finally saw her, he took her up and laid her on his shoulders, and then returned joyfully to his house.

When he got home, he brought together his family, his friends, and his neighbors. He said to them, "Come and celebrate with me! I have found the sheep I had lost, and I am so happy!"

After telling this story, Jesus said, "God is like this man. His greatest happiness is to see someone come back to him. He rejoices in that one person much more than the ninety-nine others who already believe in him."

In God's eyes, we are all valuable.
It's really comforting to know
that he takes care of us like
the shepherd in this story!

A brave shepherd

When talking about God, Jesus often told stories about everyday life. These stories were easier to understand than long speeches! Back then, there were many wild animals and thieves wandering on the roads, so a shepherd who went to look for a lost sheep risked his life! This shepherd was ready to do anything to save his sheep...

I really want to go somewhere else!

A persistent shepherd

Jesus told this story to show that everyone is precious in the eyes of God. God searches for those who wander away from him. This is exactly what Jesus did when he spoke to sinners. They felt rejected by the Pharisees and the scribes who were "proper" people. But Jesus was interested in them, he talked with them, and he cared about them.

I'm so happy to see you again!

BAAA

A good shepherd

When the shepherd found his sheep, he didn't even think of scolding or punishing her. Instead, he took her in his arms, and he was so happy to bring her home that he threw a party! Jesus does the same. He approaches sinners without judging them, telling them how glad God would be if he was reunited with them. But he does not forget the others. He explains to them that they just need him a little less because they already trust him.

The Two Houses

From the Gospel of Saint Luke, chapter 6, verses 47-49

Jesus wanted his disciples to understand that it is not enough to just listen to his words. His teachings must be put into practice. So he told them...

Every man who hears my words and
acts on them is like a man who
built his house by digging deep into the
ground and laying the foundations of his
house on a rock. When the water rose,
the torrent rushed up against the house,
but it could not be destroyed because
it was well built.

But every man who hears my words
and does not put them into practice
is like a man who built his house on
sand, without foundations. When
the water rose up, the torrent dashed
against the house, and at once it
collapsed. It was completely
destroyed.

Through this story,
Jesus invites us to seek out
what is essential to build
our lives...

Build on stone or on sand?

To tell us about our lives, Jesus used the image of two houses. On the surface, the houses may be similar. But in fact, one of the two is fragile. In our lives, it is almost the same: we often try to build our lives on temporary or artificial things like money, power, popularity, or glory. All these things are tempting because they are pleasurable. But they are also very fragile: they can slip between our fingers and disappear...like sand!

For true happiness, you must dig!

Jesus does not forbid us to enjoy life's happy moments, but he tells us that true happiness requires more effort. He asks us to dig deeply, to look for what gives meaning to life: sharing, consolation, forgiveness, love, prayer, working to make the world better... This kind of happiness is more demanding, but Jesus tells us that it is also deeper.

The strength to weather storms...

By following him, Jesus suggests that we base our happiness on something solid that can withstand storms. For he is always with us, even in challenging situations. This does not mean that we will never suffer or that we will never have trouble. But we will always be able to lean on Jesus and rely on his strength to endure the storms of life.

The Humble and the Pretentious

From the Gospel according to Saint Luke, chapter 18, verses 9-14

Some men who listened to Jesus were convinced that they were right and proper. They trusted in themselves and despised others. So Jesus told them this story...

Two men went up to the Temple to pray.
One was a Pharisee, the other a
tax collector.

The Pharisee stood there and prayed, "My God,
I thank you because I am not like other men. I am
neither a thief, nor unjust, nor adulterous. And I am
not like that tax collector. I fast twice a week and give
a tenth of all I earn as an offering to the Temple."

The tax collector stood at a distance and did not even
dare raise his eyes to heaven, but he struck his breast,
saying, "My God, have mercy on me, a sinner." When
the tax collector returned home, it was he, I tell you,
who was blessed, and not the Pharisee.
He who exalts himself will be humbled; he who humbles
himself will be exalted.

With this parable, Jesus invites us to think about what it means to be "righteous," which means to truly follow God.

What's a Pharisee?
A tax collector?

In the time of Jesus, the Pharisees were Jewish people who strove to be faithful to the law of Moses. They followed every single religious rule to the letter. The tax collectors collected the taxes for the Romans, who had taken over the country back then. Many tax collectors took some extra money to put in their pockets, which is why people didn't like them.

Law or faith?

In this parable, the Pharisee follows the law, but he does it out of duty. He is pretentious and pleased with himself, thinking he is better than everyone else. Instead of praying and reflecting on his life, he seems to say to God, "Look at how good I am! Congratulate me!" The tax collector does not lead a great life, but he dares to show himself to God as he is.

An honest portrait

This parable asks us to be honest with ourselves too, and invites us to truly turn to God with all our hearts. Jesus tells us that the most important thing is knowing how to recognize our mistakes with humbleness, and wanting to change for the better.

Sharing Talents

From the Gospel according to Saint Matthew, chapter 25, verses 14-30

One day, to explain to
his disciples how God
puts his trust in people,
Jesus said to them...

Before going on a journey, a man called his servants together to entrust his fortune to them.

To the first servant he gave five talents, that is, thirty thousand pieces of gold. To the second servant he gave two talents. And to the third servant he entrusted one talent. Each one received an amount according to his abilities.

Once the master left, the first servant began to work. He worked so hard and so well that he earned five more talents. The second also worked and earned two more talents. But the third buried the talent he had received very deeply in the earth.

A long while later, the master returned from traveling and summoned his servants to him.

The first servant came forward and handed a purse to his master, saying, "You had given me five talents. Here are five more that I earned."

"Well done!" the master exclaimed, "You are a good servant. Come and rejoice with me!"

The second servant then stepped forward and said, "Master, you gave me two talents. I earned two more!"

"Well done!" the master replied, "you are a good servant. Come and rejoice with me!"

Then the third servant, the one who buried his talent in the earth, came forward to explain to his master. He held out his talent, saying, "I was too afraid of you. I preferred to hide your money. Here it is back."

But the master was unhappy. "You are nothing but a lazybones! Why didn't you at least put my money in a bank? I would have had more when I returned!"

The master then gave the talent to the one who already had ten. And he chased away the third servant.

Jesus calls us to live the Gospel fully, for it is the best way to find happiness.

A real treasure

A talent was a coin used in the days of Jesus. A talent was a real fortune, worth seventeen years of work! But beware, Jesus did not tell this story to say we should get more and more money. He also didn't want to say that the rich are the best!

To work!

In this parable the master represents God, and the servants represent each one of us. The treasure that God entrusts to us is his Word. Everyone, no matter where we are in life, is called to live the Gospel and make it grow. Love, forgiveness, and trust are all gifts that God gives us. They are free for us to use, or not. But this parable says, if you take a chance in putting the Gospel into practice, you will inevitably win.

The adventure of life

When we receive a gift, the best way to thank the person who offered it is to use it. The third servant gave back his gift without making use of it. He did not recognize the gift God gave him, so he could not do anything with it. He shut himself off from everything because he was afraid of committing himself and taking risks to live the Gospel. And he ended up all alone. This is what made him unhappy.

The Prodigal Son

From the Gospel according to Saint Luke, chapter 15, verses 11-32

Jesus told this story:
A man had two sons. The
younger one said to his father:
"Give me my share of the
inheritance." And the father
shared his money.

A few days later, the son, having gathered all he had, went to a distant country. He spent all his money there having a good time.

Then a great famine arrived in the country, and the young man lost everything. He hired himself out to a man who sent him to feed his pigs. The son was so hungry he wanted to fill his own belly with the pigs' food, but no one gave him any. He said to himself,

"How many of my father's workers have as much bread as they want, while here I am dying of hunger! I'm going to go back to my father and say, 'Father, I have sinned against heaven and against you. I no longer deserve to be called your son. Treat me like one of your workers.'" And so he went to join his father.

While he was still far away, his father saw him on the road, and was filled with pity. He ran to him and put his arms around him and kissed him tenderly. The son said to him, "Father, I have sinned against heaven and against you, and I no longer deserve to be called your son." But the father said to his servants,

"Quickly, bring out our most beautiful robe and put it on him. Put a ring on his finger and sandals on his feet. Go and get the fatted calf, kill it, and let us eat and celebrate, for my son who was dead has come back to life! He was lost and he is found again!"

And they began to celebrate.

Meanwhile, the older son was in the fields. When he came back to the house, he heard music and people dancing. Calling one of the servants, he asked what was going on. The servant replied, "Your brother has returned, and your father killed the fatted calf because he is back safe and sound." The older son then became angry and refused to come inside to the party.

His father went out to plead with him, but he said to his father, "I always did what you wanted without ever disobeying you, and you never even gave me a young goat to eat with my friends, but when this son of yours comes back, who wasted your money, you kill the fatted calf for him!"

The father explained to him, "My child, you are always with me, and all that belongs to me is yours. But we have to celebrate and rejoice, because this brother of yours was dead, and he returned to life. He was lost, and was found again!"

With this parable,
Jesus speaks of how
God forgives and
loves us all.

Always welcome!

In this story, the father is God. And when we walk away from God, we are the son who left. Jesus wants to show us that God is like a very generous father, full of love, who rejoices when one of his children decides to return to him.

Lost and found

The father did not stop his son from leaving him. When he was far away, the father was certainly worried, but he was not going to go after him. He let his son be free. And when his son returned, he ran to kiss him, without asking for explanations or apologies. He even threw a party! Because God's forgiveness is beyond our hopes and dreams. It is limitless! But to be forgiven, God needs us to decide to come back to him first.

A place for everyone

And what about the oldest son who stayed with his father and who didn't disobey him? There's no party for him! In reality, this son received far more than a feast, because all that his father owns is his. Maybe he didn't understand that his father loved him with the same love as his brother. God loves everyone equally, but he has a thousand ways of showing it.

The Good Samaritan

From the Gospel according to Saint Luke, chapter 10, verses 29-37

In the Bible, it says,
"Love your neighbor as yourself."
But who is our neighbor? Jesus,
who was asked this question,
answered with a story...

A man was walking from Jerusalem to Jericho. On the way there, he was attacked by bandits who stole everything he had and beat him. Then they left him there half dead.

A priest passed by.
He saw the man, avoided him, and continued on his way.
A servant of the Temple passed by.
He saw the man. He also avoided him, and continued on his way.
A third man then came along.
He was a traveler from Samaria, a "Samaritan."
When he saw the man, he was moved with pity.
He went up to him and treated his wounds with oil and wine.
Then he put him onto his donkey.
He took him to an inn and watched over him.
The next day he gave two silver coins to the innkeeper, saying,
"Take care of him, and if you spend more money, I will repay you on my return."

When Jesus finished his story, he turned to the man
who questioned him and asked, "In your opinion, who
of the three travelers was the victim's neighbor?"
The man answered, "The one who had pity."
Jesus then said, "Go, and do as he did."

With this parable,
Jesus speaks to us about
how we should love our
neighbor.

A shocking story!

At the time of Jesus, the Jews of Judea and Galilee hated the Samaritans, because they believed they were unfaithful to God. But the Jews greatly admired the priests and servants of the Temple. This story, where a Samaritan is the good guy and the religious men are the bad guys, was very shocking to them!

A thorny situation

In this story, the priest and the servant of the Temple followed Jewish law very carefully. According to the law, if they touched a dead man, they would be unclean for seven days. In order to not break the law, they avoided the man lying on the ground because they believed he was almost dead. Plus, it was a place full of bandits, and they could have been attacked too. The situation was doubly dangerous!

Listen to your heart

When the Samaritan saw this man in distress, he wanted to help him. Listening to his heart, he ignored the law and his fear of bandits. Through this story, Jesus said that obeying the law or religious rules should never hold us back from really loving with the generosity, courage, and freedom of the Samaritan.

The Last-Minute Workers

From the Gospel according to Saint Matthew, chapter 20, verses 1-16

To talk about how God loves all people,
Jesus told this story to his disciples...

The kingdom of God is like a vineyard owner who came out of his house one morning, and went to the village square to find workmen for the day.
"I have work in my vineyard," he said. "I'll pay a piece of silver for the day. Are you interested?"
The workers said yes and went to his vineyard.

A little later in the morning, the master returned to the square and saw more people without work to do.
"Go and work in my vineyard," he suggested.
"I will pay you a just wage."
The workers said okay and went to his vineyard.

The master returned to the square at noon, then went again in the middle of the afternoon. Each time he found new workers. In the evening, when the day was almost over, he went one last time to the square.
Seeing the people sitting there, he asked them,
"Why did you stay here all day?"
"No one has offered us work," they replied.
Then the master sent them to his vineyard.

Night fell at the end of the day. The master of the vineyard called all his workers together to pay them. He started with those who arrived last and gave each one a piece of silver. Seeing this, the other workers were excited, saying to themselves, "If they got one piece of silver, then we will get even more!" But the master also gave them the same amount.

Then one of them got angry. "Those guys who worked just an hour earned the same as us who sweated all day?"

The master replied, "My friend, I did not wrong you! I promised you a just wage, right? So take it and go home. If I want to give to someone as much as I gave to you, does that take something away from you? Why are you jealous when I am generous?"

Does God love everyone in the same way? This is the great question Jesus asks when he tells this parable...

56

The parables are wonderful stories!

In the days of Jesus, storytellers and teachers often used parables. These are short stories where the meaning is explained at the end. The parables seem simple because they talk about fields, vineyards, trees, and animals. But to understand the message behind them, sometimes you have to think pretty hard!

Who's who?

In this parable, the master of the vineyard is God, and we are the workers. Some people are like the first workers of the narrative: they met God very early and served him from the first hour. Others are more like the last workers: they spent much of their life away from God, and only discovered him very late.

Enough love for everyone!

With this parable, Jesus tells us that all people don't meet God at the same time. But God welcomes us all in the same way, whether we come to him first or last. It is never too late to meet God, because all of his love is there for each one of us!

Salt and Light

From the Gospel according to Saint Matthew, chapter 5, verses 13-16

And now for some salt...

Yum!

Jesus went up on a mountain,
and when he sat down,
his disciples came to him.
Here's what he said on that day...

You are the salt of the earth! But what's the use of salt if it loses its taste? It would be no longer good for anything except to be thrown out and trampled by the crowd.

You are the light of the world! A city built on a hill cannot be hidden!

In the same way, we don't light a lamp to hide it! It is placed prominently on a lamppost, so that its light shines on everyone in the house.

So let your light shine in the eyes of all people! Then, seeing your good works, they will glorify your Father in heaven.

Salt that is worth gold!

In Jesus's time, salt was extremely precious. Since there were no refrigerators, salt was the only way to preserve food. Back then, salt made life possible. Jesus thus invites his disciples to share the treasure they have received, the Word of God, so that each one could live a full and happy life.

Pass it on

In this parable, Jesus encourages all of his followers to go and live out their faith wherever possible. He says to them, "Do not be afraid! Do not be ashamed!" For it is God's plan to tell each person that they are infinitely loved. But no one will know if no one talks about it! So for two thousand years, each Christian has had the task of passing on this treasure.

Make the light shine

For Jesus, it is not enough just saying you believe in him to be a shining light in the world. What does it mean to believe in him if you don't always try to move toward justice, love, peace, and forgiveness? Being a Christian means taking action in order to make the world welcoming for all.